TWO HEARTS NEVER HEAL THE SAME

(Poetry for Love & Life)

By-
Bhushan Gosavi

Introduction

Thank you for choosing this book which will give you an experience of exploring the beauty of love & loss, the mountains of strength, the oceans of darkness & hope, the infinite stars, and nights to be remembered with some heart-touching rhymes.

This book is a collection of emotions of true love, true pain, true hustle, and true story embedded in the form of poetries, prose & short stories in simple words with deep meaning!

EACH WORD WRITTEN IN THIS BOOK IS FOR "YOU" SO "READ IT FOR YOURSELF".

Whether you are on the way to building self-love, chasing your dreams, healing from your past, struggling with life, talking to yourself every day, having a Dream, & looking for perfect words to describe these emotions *"TWO HEARTS NEVER HEAL THE SAME"* will be an ideal addition to your bookshelf.

The journey is about inspiring to be grateful for one's past and describing the nature of life with the power of self-love dedicated to a Dream. You are about to create something Magical, just like Me, you are on your Dream, which has brought you here with me...!!

Welcome Home!!

I never thought I could write, but then Life happens…
I hope you enjoy reading this book as much as I did writing it for you.

-All my Love

THIS BOOK HAS 4 CHAPTERS:

1) FIRE HEART

2) BLEED LOVE

3) SOMETHING FOR YOU

4) THIS IS FOR YOU

A POET, AN ANOTHER LIFE!!

Table of Contents

FIRE HEART

FIRE

Feels like the world is just gold
& the Heaven could also be blue
Holding something in me here,
Every day I grew!!

Meeting so many humans
Spreading love on my way,
But all I did for them
Made me really stay
Secretly, but to this day!

Sometimes I think
Is this their blessing,
Or the power in me
which I needed for rising?

Realizing my inner soul
Was the only thing I did,
I never knew this
When I was once a little kid

So amazing is this life
Grateful every day to my Lord,
Which made me strive a lot
Turning the game into an odd

I always believed in myself
One day will be mine,
and on that day
I will beautifully shine..
Still, Life is so big
I will give my whole,
One day! I'll achieve my goal
Because,
I got FIRE in my soul...!!
Now, Let it burn..!!

INSIDE ME I HOLD

Walking this life
Some new & some old,
Nowadays there's something
Inside me I hold

Mind full of thoughts
Plated with the color of gold,
Playing with them daily
Something in me I hold

Things remained unsaid
While memories are still unsold,
Memoriesss! OMG!
So many of them I hold

Feelings left unfelt
Through this severe cold,
Blessed with those feelings
Something inside me I hold

Trusting this path
While some days remain untold,
Every day I believed in
That thing which I hold

A beautiful view of life
With millions of moments rolled,
Recalling those moments
Something in me I hold

Days be so busy
But still, I love to write bold
I think this is my blessing
Because yes, something Inside me I HOLD..!! ♥

DID YOU NOTICE?

Did you notice?
Heart said Hello
To a stranger passing by....
Not with a smile
Nor with a hieee
Just with some good vibes &
A crazy imagination, oh why?
What was in the past?
What is in the present?
Millions of emotions
This little heart has spent....
This little heart has spent....
So much of time
It's too tough to understand
Whether I was yours
or you were mine?
Violets are a little blue, & the sky is sometimes yellow
You are my moon now.
And I'm just a street fellow..
Now my day doesn't end
Without seeing the moon,
Waiting for it all-day
Hoping to end this soon....
A feeling of the twisted ride
Which takes me back home,
Remembering so many things
Like a lovely syndrome

So did you notice?
Heart said Hello
To a stranger passing by...
I think I was too high
To let it all go..!!

"Some stories never end....
They just have to end to start a new story..!!"

BE LIKE A BIRD

In a world of everything fancy
It's time to fly high,
Far away somewhere
Until we reach the sky

Keeping yourself a little bit up
From the things that let you down,
Will keep you going, my friend
Just like a life's rebound

The days you were alone
Alone to be known,
Is just like the chocolate ice-cream
Extreme sweetness, but not in the cone!!

Looking normal but thinking deep
As you sow, so shall you reap,
It's better to know what to keep
Is the Life's beautiful tip

Living twice in each moment
Never knowing the end,
Feels like something is coming &
A new life is about to begin

The sky is your limit
Just like a free bird flying,
Trying to reach somewhere
Forgiving so many things

Trust your intuition of love
Keeping faith in your Heart and your Word,
Just keep flying and searching
The lovely dream of the Flying Bird
What could it be?
BE LIKE A BIRD ❤

I HAD A DREAM

I had a dream
Don't know if it will come true,
Because it's the only time nowadays
When I find you!

I had a dream
As I have every night,
We sitting on a hilltop
Holding each other so tight!

I had a dream
We were lying down,
Somewhere on a silent seashore
So away from our hometown

I had a dream
We walked on the country streets,
Didn't care about anyone
While you looked so sweet

I had a dream
A future of us so bright,
But we both made mistakes
And then I had to write

I had a dream
It's hard to convey,
Words are turning less &
I am on my way

Yes, I like to see
A lot of dreams,
With one as a hope to complete
The incomplete WE..!!

Maybe Someday..!!

CITY LOVE

In this beautiful city,
I believe..

The moon has its place..
Where it lives and takes some rest,
Every night it comes out at its best,
Nowhere but in this wonder quest..
With its presence,
When Love plays its role
Millions of emotions grow..
While some feelings are sown..

In this beautiful city
I believe..
When the wind blows,
It carries an essence..
An essence of some memories
And pretty moments in a row,
Some just get lost
While I go with the flow..

In this beautiful city
I believe,
We Live, Laugh, and Love..
Always ready for what's coming,
& also for the much-needed dove,
Enjoying this present
Do not care a bit about
The times when we get low,
& times when we get high
Because one day you know,
We all gonna surely die!

In this beautiful city
I believe,
We always try to live different versions of ourselves…
Sailing in the same boat,
Of madness and depth..
Not knowing a bit about
our beloved destinations..

We just flow and flow..
In this beautiful city with our lovely dreams..!!

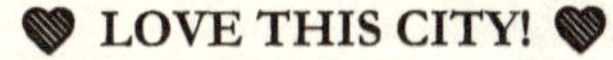

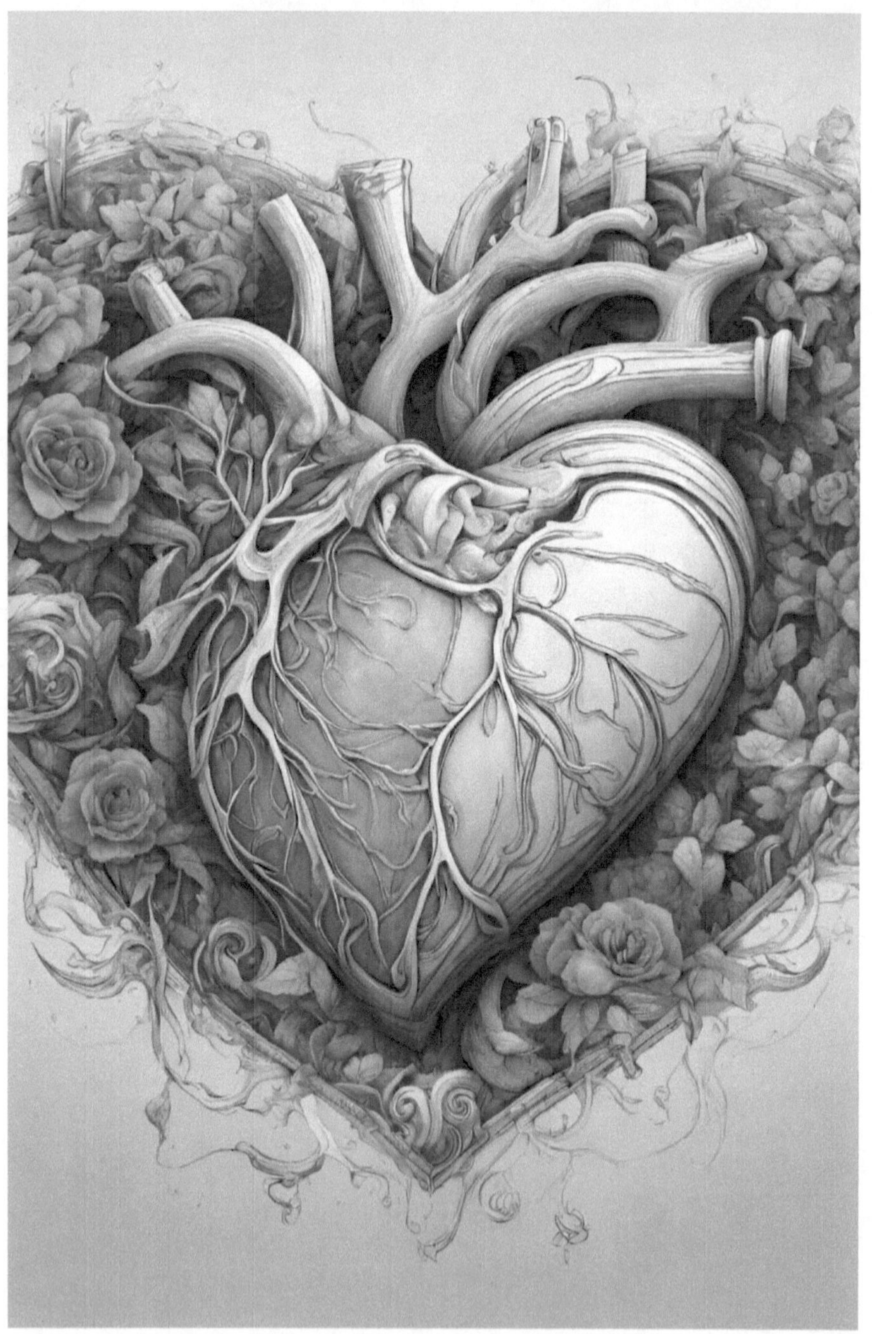

A POET'S HEART

In this huge world
Thousand miles apart,
All that keeps us connected
Is a precious Heart..!!

It's a beautiful God Gift &
A sign of love,
Everyone is lucky
I am blessed to have one

Feels a lot
Broken many times,
We have our tune
And our magical rhymes

Even if I feel
Happy or sad,
Together we share this feeling
No matter how good or bad

Does many things
Which are not its part,
Still, no one can ever judge
The Power of a Heart..

All I have inside, Deep down in me
Comes from you, which only I can see

Now if I decide to stop
I know you'll make me start,
Because deep down I know
The real VALUE OF MY HEART..!! 🖤

DO YOU??

EVOLUTION

You keep walking
You keep fighting,
But the real magic lies
In none other than living...!!

Living the days you could
Surviving the days you couldn't,
Be proud of who you are
Right now, in this moment!

Moments, they form golden memories
Which will take you so far,
Be it in your mind or your heart
Feeling like you are on the seventh star...

The journey of this path
Will drown you sometimes,
Either in love or in yourself
Giving you a reason every time

Time is a treasure here
It never returns or comes back,
We have to live with it
And rest is just the playback

Everyone lives & everyone goes wrong
Life is meant for it,
But what matters the most is
What do you do to survive from it...

The mathematics of this equation
Will always be in your name,
The stronger mind of EVOLUTION
Determines Who wins the Game..!!

HARD WORK

It all starts from
A life's birth
On this beautiful planet
We call it Earth!

Growing and glowing
Learning through life
Each one has its own,
Reason to survive

I have found mine
Maybe yours is still unknown,
Do you remember that race?
In which the tortoise finally won...

Each one is running here
With a hope in their heart to win,
But only you know
Up to where you have been...

Trusting yourself
Walking towards the goal,
Maybe one day you can achieve
What you speak to your soul.....!!!!

The clock keeps ticking
Until one reaches its time
Even if fallen several times
Be ready again, to climb

In this life like a boss
Why live as a normal clerk?
Keep on going, my friend
Just keep up the HARD WORK!

YOU CAN DO IT..!! 

"Yesterday, Today, Tomorrow
We always talk with a person
Not with any physical being but
Someone,
Unknown, unfound, magical!
A person who owes you,
A person who chooses you,
A person who is always there with you,
A person who knows all kinds of you,
Sometimes I think we are living two lives,
The present physical one and the one inside us,
We are so fortunate for this miracle,
To happen to us...
Enjoy every moment of it,
Who knows when this will end
Because Miracles are on our way!
As always!
Living one of them!!

called LIFE"

FEELING (Sonnet)

A little complete,
A little incomplete
Yes, this is me, A Feeling!

Mostly unpredictable but mixed
I would rather be in someone's soul,
Rather than with one's heart & mind...

I dream of being satisfied, every time I come out of a soul,
But I am worried about being unfelt and staying forever,

I am the start of everything with a positive vibe
No, I don't have a life to stay awake late at nights
The best thing I have done so far is,
Chose life to live & survive
And the worst,
Cannot be explained in anything!!!

I feel guilty, sometimes for going on to the wrong path without any destination,

But time is my best friend be it night or day,
I think, if I didn't exist this could be a fully numb world, oh yeah!

Lastly,
I would like to be remembered as the essence of the seventh color in the rainbow!
Faded but felt...

Yes, I am a FEELING ❤

BEAUTIFUL LOVE

It's said, in this whole world
There's so much beauty,
Nah! No one like you
You hold the tag "Cutie"

There's so much to look
Above in those blue skies,
But my heaven is right there
In those magical eyes..!!

A spark that shines
Lighting up your face,
Words are few
To describe that chase

Didn't know something was hidden
In that beautiful smile,
Which made me happy
And free for a little while

So hurtful is this life &
So do your byes, darling,
They tell a few secrets
With some painful lies

Don't know what to say
& how you came my way,
So lucky I feel
My dear, I want you to stay

So blessed are you
With the beauty of your own
God creates miracle
By creating You he has Shown...!! ♥

HE-ART HEART..!!

On these vast lands
So many humans out there,
With a pumping organ
Many of them don't know...
Why it is, or for whom?
Missing life's secret,
Yes, I am talking about the HEART.... ♥

Which sets you apart
From the wildness of this globe,
Because it's only yours
Not always but sometimes...
Living a puzzled life,
Struggling from the past
Proving yourself every time
Even when not asked......
Carrying inside a pain,
We came out of nothing,
Never thought of this moment
This is just the Rising...!!
Blessed are we,
Everyone with their uniqueness
Keep shining my Hogwarts buddies
There is always nothing less...!!
We are here for a purpose
And so do I,
Creating art, just by writing my heart,
There's no end here, this is just a start
The art of writing...
Taught the secret of life,
I am grateful every day for the change
Always rocking in a higher range,
Did you know?
All that lies is the magic
in the word, HEART,

"HE stands for me
& Art just for you"

Walking in a miracle
In the dream of some remembered nights
Talking with you and your heart
Under the moon's dim light….
All this is pure Magic...!!!!
Just gone within the blink of an eye
You're lucky if you realize,
Why did the night turn so bright?
The Art keeps it alive
Even if it is rough,
There is nothing greater, than your dreams….
Keep chasing and walking this game
Which is a mixture of love & hate,
The hard work will pay off one day
Until you win my mate!!

I am the Real Hero here,
Everything is just inside me,
Praising and writing a legacy
With all My Heart and My Art !!

This is HE-ART ♥

REAL FREEDOM

Once it's easy,
And sometimes complicated,
Feels a little confused
And mostly out of your head

The days we live in silence
All alone without anyone,
These are the days that will show you
You are Something & Someone!

Life takes a new turn
Taking you to an unknown destination,
But in the end, everything is peaceful
All that matters is your attention

These are the times when
You will explore a new dimension of life,
For the things which you've been doing
& the moments from the past which you lived in

Being trapped in the shadows of the dark
It's time to search for the spark left behind,
Just believing in yourselves
Will lead you to that one-of-a-kind...

This chapter of newness
Will never turn too old,
It will be remembered forever
Just like you discover the real Gold!!!

Yes, the Real Gold is in You, my friend...
Always treasure these days,
When you meet yourself with
Some unknown hidden ways

Keep walking this way,
You never know where you could reach
Nor do you know its end
It's a heaven-calling trip

Just wondering how was life,
Back then few years before
I am still dancing here, in my own melody
Because there's a lot left on the floor...!!

YOU ARE DIFFERENT

Living this life
Which is just like an ocean wave,
You still have the spark in you
Yes, You are Different

Hundreds of things going on
In this busy mind,
Don't know which is the current
But yes, You are Different

Feeling low sometimes
Sometimes higher than life,
You always try to be vociferant
Yes, You are Different

The puzzle of being lost
Is so difficult to understand,
Making you a bit indifferent
But yes, You are Different

Reminiscing about those days
Which are just like a blessing now,
Never lose this interest because
Yes, You are different

The fire in your eyes
& the peace in your soul,
Makes you a little magnificent,
Yes, You are different

This story begins with You
& also ends with You
Making this birth a little significant
Because,
Yes, You are Different & You matter...!! ♥

"A dream,
A dream is flying'
Far away in the blues'
With the lovely breezes, on the surface of oceans...
While behind those mountains
Singing with the birds, sometimes aiming at the moon,
In the unsteady minds,
Overcoming the painful grounds
A dream is flying'
With love & magic around!
Believing this thought...
and the things we live...
Creating a belief to touch the sky
While holding a lot to give,
We never think much but we do dream! ??
A dream,
A dream is flying' somewhere
In which we Live 'in!! "

WRITE

What a beautiful day….
with the shining sun
An interesting story is this,
Life's amazing run

Have you ever wondered?
About the bleeding hearts
Of those green trees
Which had already fallen apart

The birds sing, a song so loud
Watching their gifted wings, makes one feel proud

This sky is so eternal
Holding a million stars,
But no one ever knew
It's beautiful scars...

The night is talking, with the glowing moon
All I wished if, I could touch it soon...

Life seems better now
With a proper balance,
All that helped me
Is my only friend, Silence!

Staying in peace
With a hopeful future bright,
Some lines by this red heart
Because it loves to WRITE!

Yes, it's Writing
Yes, it Writes...!! ♥

FRANKLIN GOT LOST!!

In this world
With millions of people around,
Everyone is struggling with their life
Surrounding with some broken hearts

With so many reasons
Each one trying to live,
Carrying the peaceful hurt in themselves
Trying to just believe

I wonder just to believe
Where they started from, till the end....
Sometimes I think people feel
These feelings at their backend

Fighting demons every day
Calling me to the hell of our story,
I often visit this beautiful palace
Where there is no one now & the rest is history

Sometimes I feel like I can never die
Coz I never was alive,
Searching for my loved ones
Every day, every time in my eyes
Just like a whale passing
In the ocean of lovely hopes,
This mind carries millions of thoughts
It doesn't really have any scores

Living in this world just a bit unknown
We always miss what is left behind,
With the energy to grow every time
But then life just revolves around

We are not the same as we were before
All that lies is a secret with the shore,
In this roller-coaster of mysteries
I just want to swim more, more and more!!

These are just some heartfelt lines
You could relate to something that is passed,

I am Benjamin here
& the Franklin just got lost...!!

THIS IS MY TIME!! (2:4)

This is my time
A time to find me,
To grow and learn
For a life's perfect turn

A time to find me
A time to chase hidden dreams,
For a life's perfect turn
This is what I need…

A time to chase hidden dreams
From a lonely fantasy,
This is what I need &
This is what I barely see

From a Lonely Fantasy
Emerges a new me,
This is what I barely see
So wild and so free…

Emerges a new me
In my poetic style,
So wild and so free
Very different to see for a while

In my poetic style
I'll achieve my dream,
Very different to see
Will be this magical theme?

I'll achieve my dream,
Hopefully, with a perfect rhyme
Will this be a magical theme?
Oh yes! This is my time...!!

THIS IS MY TIME! ❤

"Love the person you are becoming because the people who are not with you aren't worth the person you are becoming"

SHINING STAR

In our lovely world
we were so good together,
laughing and loving
holding each other,
so beautiful was that
Theme of life,
so strongly I believed
You will be My future wife!!

But as someone said
Life's an untold story,
Never did we knew
These feelings do get buried....

A sudden change of destiny
Took us miles away,
Now it feels so silent
The colors changed to all-grey

I am still confused baby
Regarding our play,
Words got lost &
A lot remained to say

Sometimes I wonder
Was this the Magic of God?
Which changed my life & turned it into an odd...

Now I believe in magic
Which took me so far,
One day I will be
Your favourite Shining Star...!!

KEEP SHINING...!!

LET THIS FIRE BURN!!!!

Once upon a time, while traveling alone,
Suddenly I recalled, the grateful past I own!

Days turned back, which I thought were real,
But nothing worked out, everything was ideal!

People are Poison, someone said it right
It couldn't work though, even if, I was ready to fight.

It's so sad enough, the act of giving up,
Pouring out the happiness, from life's empty cup!

Time says to stay upheld, even if it matters a lot,
Continue enjoying life, without giving it a thought!

Not everyone you lose is a loss
Always get ready for yourself, to be the new boss!

Something different is written here,
Life is about to take a turn,
With all my heart

LET THIS FIRE BURN!!
LET THIS FIRE BURN!!

BLEED LOVE

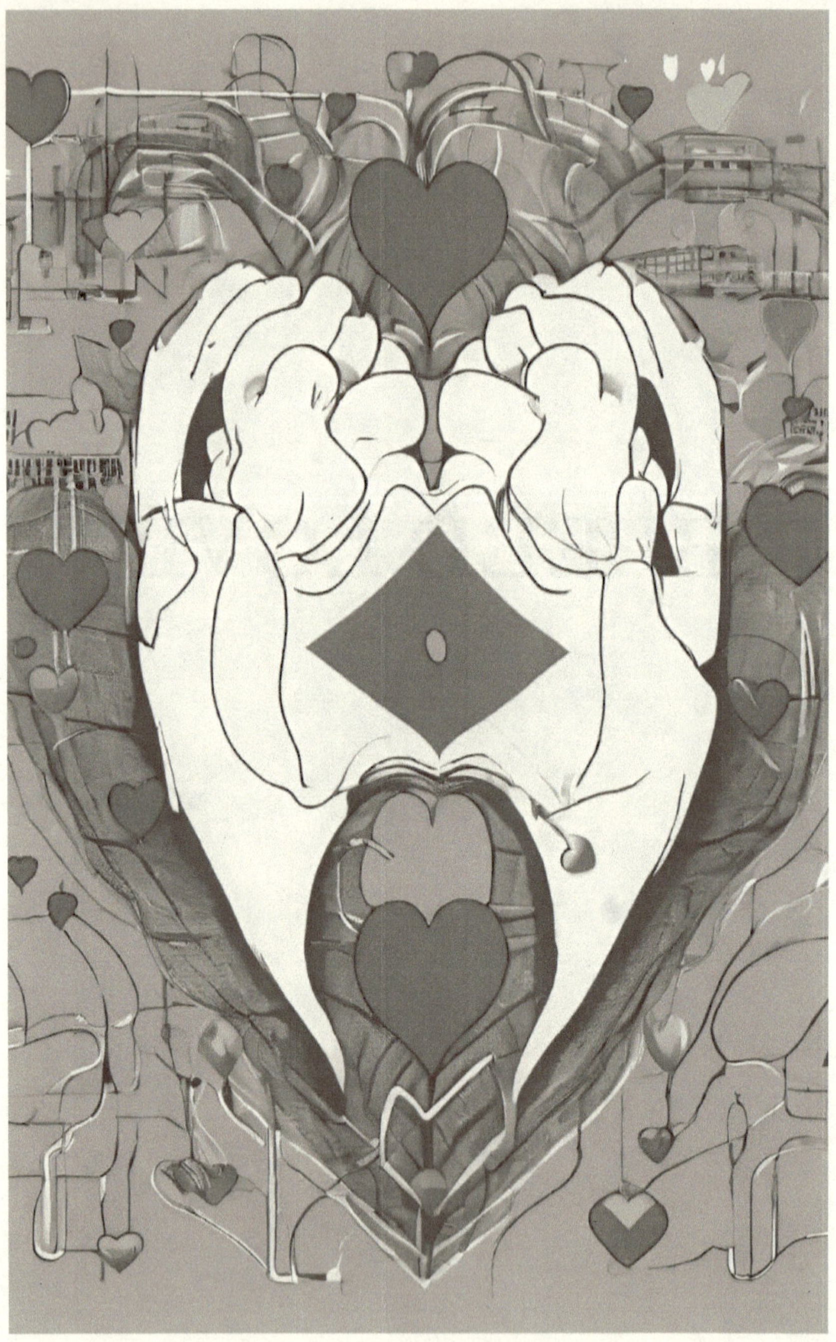

TALKING LOVE

It is too easy
To fall in me,
Perhaps very difficult
To forget me...

I give people, A reason to live,
To stay happy
Every day and every eve...

I create memories
Which are so rare
Hard to pass over,
& indescribable to share!

Some proved me true & a lot false,
Many are still in search
While some skipped the research...

No one can judge me
and my entangled mysteries...
Take a chill dude!!
They are repeated since histories

In this game
The dreams are turned,
Sometimes I am safe
Or sometimes completely burnt,

Such a magical creation,
And heaven after the deep dove
Oh gosh!
It's me here, I am "Love"...

DID WE EVER MEET? ♥

WINDSTORY

Nowadays when the wind blows...
it reminds me,
of our existence,
Deep down in a faded thought,
of being together
it takes me away,
To the place where,
we used to see the world,
in each other eyes,
Not with fire, but with a spark
Not for a moment, but forever
Though sometimes,
It aches to give up,
on such a lovely thought,
it reminds me of something,
for a little while
My heart skips a beat
Just before your smile...
Our beautiful memories,
& moments in a row...

Nowadays when the wind blows.......

MAYBE ONE DAY

Maybe one day, my mind will forget,
Your sweet name with, no reason to regret

Maybe one day, my hands won't remember,
Your heavenly touch, in the cold of December

Maybe one day, my lips won't die,
To kiss you hard & then never lie

Maybe one day, I will forget those eyes,
Staring at me, the times we said goodbyes

Maybe one day, my arms will find,
A soulmate, one of your kind

Maybe one day, my heart will be strong,
The memories you gave, will be cherished for long

Maybe one day
My soul will be free,
Sailing on this never-ending
Deep Painful Sea...

Maybe One day!!

BYE'S

In this short life
We live on so many lies,
Does anyone care?
About the remembered last BYE'S...

So, Here's something
About these byes,
Which are so mortal,
Then the beautiful Hie's

Sometimes very touchy
Sometimes not at all,
Deep inside it hurts
Why is it easy to recall?

Battles between ego, & fake promises in which,
One changes
While the other just misses!

One letter with
Three alphabets,
Can take you to places
You never thought....

A new journey begins
But so many hearts stop,
Though it's painful
Be ready to rock!

Crying eyes,
And shedding tears,
Just like the pretty pouring skies
This is all about,
Those Lost BYE's...!!

"I was walking by an empty road thinking of you,
Suddenly a cool breeze blew me away,
Since then, I understood Love was in the Air...

While I was still walking on the same road,
I am still walking...

PEOPLE DO CHANGE

Day by Day,
Month by months
They go far
and finally, part their ways...

Never did you imagine
A reason to stay,
Leaving me alone
In the Summers of May'

I never thought off
Such a puzzling game,
Now I can barely hear
Someone calling my name...

I still remember your voice
and the way we used to talk
Those rolling happy eyes,
The times we met for a walk

Some days I wondered
How people are best,
But you proved me wrong
Apart from all the rest

Nowadays I fear people,
To get close and open up
The pretty times I did so,
My heart was broken up

Giving life lessons,
With a perfect range
Someone said it right back then
PEOPLE DO CHANGE...

YES, THEY DO!!

LOST LOVE

It was me, I was myself
Then pierced a needle,
All of a sudden in the middle

Nothing to lose, either to gain
A lost paradise, Full of pain!

Neither I changed, Nor I was gone
It was silent baby,
The game was always on...

Then your absence was very rare
But deep down, I could hardly care…

Melting feelings with a broken heart
But darling!
You were already apart!!

Never will you find
One of my kind
so, Cheers to our life &
To the memories left behind

Now, in the winter snow
& in the first rain
Only the Almighty knows
When we will meet AGAIN? :')

2016

Don't know who invented the concept,
Of these past years,
I wished everything could disappear
& just never come
Because most years are amazing but
Remembered are only some!

Don't you agree...??

So, this year started with
Good hope and smile,
Things running fine
Felt calm for a while...

But after some days
Suddenly life changed,
Learning a lot each day
Thoughts got engaged,
Engaged & lost in some world
Which handled this theme,
Surviving from it
I could only let my feelings scream...

As time flew
Work turned out to be my friend,
And thus, I became comfortable
With this new trend

Lots of things
A year can hold,
These are the secrets
That can never be told...

Now, If I live for years or die as a teen
Most happening year of my life,
Will always be 2016...!! ❤

"In a field of green grass
We lay under the blue infinite sky
She said she is like a jackfruit
Rigid outside, sweet inside,
I said, oh Darling why so?
My hand was her pillow
Had a red rose design on it
She said, eat me,
I said, of course, but
I am afraid of love"

BROKEN CASTLE

The things that we did for people
And the promises we made,
Somewhere it all stays back
In a place unsaid

Walked so far under the almighty sky
It took us miles away
Now I am in love with it
Be it anywhere or any day

So sweet was that
Amazing atmosphere
My heart just beat once
And you were already here

Time was love, Love was time
When I was yours & You were mine!

But clocks do spin
So do the situations,
Feelings suddenly disappeared
Into the deep dark oceans

A place where it left
Will always be unknown,
Though the path was painful
Today there's something of me that I own…

For once I felt like
I was in a hustle
To discover this
New BROKEN CASTLE...!!

Where once we met happily
But I loved to Travel...!!

"In the forest of roses
There were so many thorns
I was,
Walking, searching
A color of infinity in them
The touch of the sweet smell
Reminding that swell
Finally, I found a Rose!
In which I felt myself
When I bought it, I realized
Flowers do get old & dry
So why should I not give it a try
Amongst many different flowers of love
So beautiful!
I was searching for a mixture of
A little you &
A little me"

THE DAY SHE LEFT

The Day she left
She was looking so sweet,
But slowly days turned after that last meet…

The day she left
Was full of hope
Though the love was half
There was a little scope

The day she left
Was so silent and calm
Though it was hard
I felt, we still had that charm to go on & on
But,

The day she left
Feelings got lost
Being together in one soul
Is love free of cost??

The day she left
Was the day love died
I was broken, my heart cried….

The day she left
Was like a nightmare
I almost survived, which was too hard to bear

The day she left
Is so hard to forget
Almighty is watching
I hope, one day she will regret...
Because this love is so true
She failed to know it
Although her Romeo had died,
She was my Real Juliet, which I had…

The day she left
Looking at the moon, I thought
Maybe in my life's paragraph,
She was just a tiny dot…

Maybe this is why
I am writing my RIGHT,
Mind flying so high
Since THE DAY SHE LEFT!

ENDLESS

Days pass with
The heart we carry,
It looks so blissful behind
A Faded Memory!

Eyes say they look
A very different sky,
Maybe a little brighter
Paradise so high

Dreams meet the tune
Of the passing time,
With a hope to write
Some beautiful, heart-touching lines!

Maybe the winds
Take me to a place,
To the backyard of memories
Where nothing is just the same

So huge is this world in which
A little life is so fine
I survived my lonely days
Just with some liquor & cold wine

For the sleepless nights
& the complex mind thinking,
There are many ways
Which one can heal in
Short but sweet,
Some day when My story Ends'
More and more
Hearts it will mend! ❤

THIS IS ENDLESS!!

DID YOU KNOW?

Did you know?
You would ever come?
In this weird poet's life
And just never go

Did you ever know?
About my heart
Which always loved you
Baby, only you were its part

Do you remember?
The moments which we spent
In search of true love
Even if we tried, they would never end

Did you ever know?
My love for you
Yes, it was forever
Up above beyond the blues

Did you know?
We would die for each other
Living our life happily
Just with one another

Did you know?
You were the burning fire
In my heart
Now, turning into a lovely desire!

Do you remember?
The love that we craved
For years and forever
Don't know why, but,
I will surely make it stay...!!

DID YOU KNOW??

"......A night,
That changed my universe
Beautifully with grace
Where the shattered stars of gold
Are still trying to uphold...
A ray of light
Taking the hope so high
Just like a coconut tree
Free, tall, and independent
I searched the ray between its sheds
Till the night turned up
Telling me to stay awake
To see the stars ache
Running into the room
I cried a lot,
For the love of the sky,
Holding a thought
Trying to stop the night,
Which was Dark and silent
Just like the obnoxious nature of life someday"

WE ALL ARE BROKEN!!

In the era of love
Sometimes we burn,
And sometimes we heal
But what's left is
Just some memories to take a feel...

We live on memories,
We live on moments rather,
I will never forget that time
When we were apart but together

The past is full of smiles
But now I wander for happiness,
Don't know about the future
But hoping to achieve a little success

Thanks for this blessing, O Lord,
Now I am chasing a dream
Feelings are just like flights,
Nowadays they do not have fins

Vibing higher!!
I don't care about the present,
Some things made me feel alive
When I was just absent

Just like a monk, I sit here
To explore and touch myself
Though it's a tough journey,
Always remember to love yourself
This is the Magic of life
Which needed a lot, just to happen
Surviving through the wave of it
I know, WE ALL ARE BROKEN,

Yeah, we all are a little broken...!! ❤

LOST SOULS...!!

In a matter of fire,
Or in a glimpse of light…
They see everything
Yes, their future is bright!

Traveling around the world
With a mind full of different keys
Even if lost sometimes
The heart sees, what it sees

Oh! But it does not have eyes
Maybe it all lives in the skies,
Connecting to the universe
Outside your body which never dies

Cheers to such people!
Who live a life full of mysteries
Celebrating Memories!
& Creating Histories!!

Struggling through the odds
Standing with the even
How does it feel to be given?
Then, searching for our heaven

Doing what feels right,
Just by heart or ways apart
Sometimes overcoming the past
Is the most beautiful Art...!!

Hiding but yet want to be seen
With a heart full of love,
Now, let the secrets redeem
Something for the "LOST SOULS"

THE FEELING OF MISSING!

What does it take to remind?
What does it take to rewind...
It's all about a time
Which is all left behind

The time when all was love
The time when people were our,
When we liked to laugh
And the rest was just leftover

Our life, our period
It makes us paranoid,
For the things we did
When we used an android...

It describes a heavy heart
Which still survives from the past,
Cheers to the moments
Which we thought, would forever last

I am a lover of memories
They still pierce my heart,
It's so tough here now
Even if I decide to restart

Those vibes are recalling
I know, we are far away,
This is a game were
Even if I die tomorrow, still we both stay...

We can't get over a life
Nor we can forget the times we laughed
This FEELING OF MISSING,
Is just like a forever-saved draft!!

Yes, I love this feeling a lot! ♥

MEET TO LIFE!

Everyone has a past, full of scars and pain,
Only a few survive & love as old again...
Pain!!
It changes you but, does not change your heart,
Because the Heart holds something and sets it apart...
We grow, we learn
Through the shadows of dark,
A little bit of memories,
Still have a spark!
Remembering everything that the heart holds,
These are the things that remain untold...
Don't let these things harden your heart, for a while,
Because there's nothing great,
Just before your smile!
This bond is so different
Get away from this pain in your heart,
Because it's time for a new life to start...

Let that grow which was watered for years,

Let's get blessed with happy tears,

Let that meet which was missed...

Oh yes!
A meet to Live, A meet to life! ♥

DID YOU EVER KNOW? (PART:2)

Did you ever know?
About that thing...
Which no one ever knows
God has kept it a secret
Yes, everyone has their stories
But the secret applies to all
I know the secret,
I am the chosen one here amongst all…
We all live a life,
In a day there are 24 hours
Same planet, same universe
But each one is so diverse….
Did anyone know about their tomorrow?
Either known to some
And the rest think it's just kept
We don't know our tomorrow,
And this is the God's Secret 🖤

Did you ever know?
My birth date or never did I know yours,
Who the hell cares here
But the mind just keeps an eye
The truth is that we never knew
In a year of 365 days,
There is a day when we are born
And also, there is a date When We Die! 🖤
We all go through that date
Years by years passing,
Living life madly & fully

Living that day every year with a feeling 🖤
Don't know where we launch
In some thoughts unknown,
Do we ever think about that day?
When we all will be sown....
This is the reality,
This is the whole game,
No one is different but
Everyone has their name!
All it comes to is when,
Each one of us is gonna go
And thus, this story remains
Unknown, unfound & untold......

Did you ever know...??
Everything on this side is evergreen
Finding the depth of myself
Bcoz we live once and this life is a blessing...
We do not exist in the solar system,
But our planet does...
Living one for the planet
With a connect
Grateful every day,
Even if we don't know our last day,
So, let the good times roll & stay!! 🖤
This life is a web of faith & hopes
You can climb with golden ropes
Reaching a destination, where
There is a rainbow, so dope....
Love and love around everywhere
Felt like I was Romeo, just to bear

Did you ever know?
Well, that's upon your luck, my dear,
Lucky people here, they only live once
Riding every day in the race
In this game of life
There are no breaks....

Everything just flows, no one can stop time
Which is also a weapon,
Did you ever know?
If not, then just follow the truth....

We are so blessed to live Today!
Celebrating My Tale of Love
Which the whole world is probably,
Gonna know someday ♥ ♥ ♥ ♥

DID YOU EVER KNOW..??

SOMETHING FOR YOU

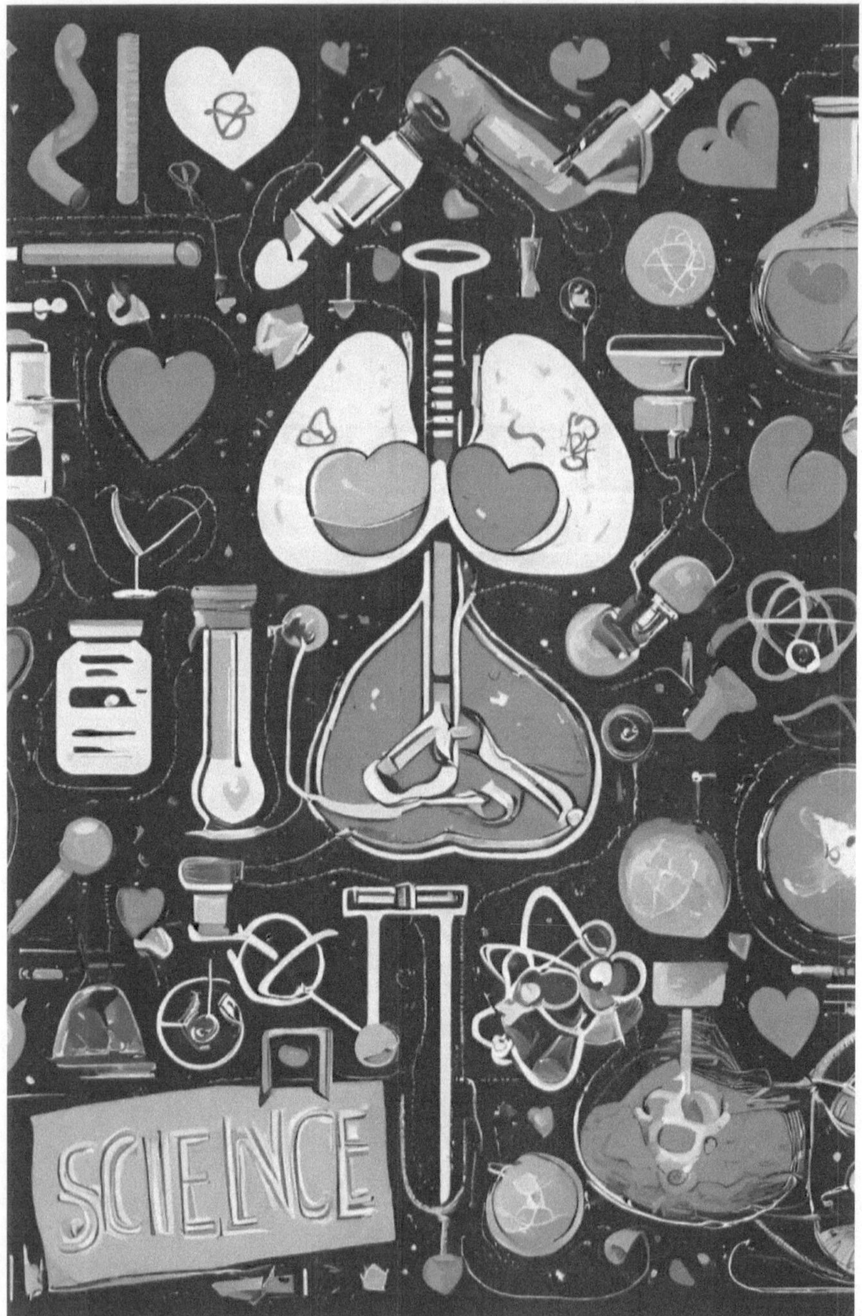
SCIENCE

SCIENCE OF LOVE

It all started in the laboratory of magic,
Where our atoms and molecules ruled the world,
We never knew any reactions,
Neither a single chemical...
But it all began,
With a chemistry
Chemistry took us away
Far somewhere in the state of acids
Ready to burn,
Ready to react,
Ready to create,
To create something different &beautiful!
Fumes of love spread all over
With the shiny spark when We both met,
Water knew our reality, some in the form of tears...
While Oxygen helped us to burn, without any fear,

In the physics of our dreams then,
We matched the speed so well...
Knowing there is a flow after every resistance,
Ringing our Love bell!!
Gravity pulled us together
With the love meter in our hands,
Fixing high frequency was the thing we did,
In our little castle of sand...
As the sand dunes attracted,
& So did our entwined hearts...!!

The biological flow of love,
Don't know was the story or just a part...
The genes and hormones,
Began to sing a song...
We never knew this kingdom

Would grow so strong...!!
The cell membrane began to dance
With the perfect energy so far
then transforming memories
In many vitamins scars
scars formed a syndrome
which grew a lot
forming a hierarchy
with a voluntary shot…

But in this laboratory of Magic, as they say
Anything can happen any day
One can survive so far
Or just fade away someday...
Trying to describe a Science of our love,
which I thought was not so rough...
I never knew this science,
Could be so tough,
Could be so tough,
Could be so tough...!!

JOURNEY

Somewhere Me
Somewhere You,
Everyone here
Is in the queue

Queue or journey
There's always a glitch,
But in the end, what matters
It is where you reach...

Old music playing
In the new mind,
Dancing memories with them
There's yet a lot to rewind

From an unknown past
To a known present,
It describes everything
What was to be meant

Changing a little self with the unstoppable time
Still, this heart remains real,
The mind chooses to wander
But I choose to be ideal

This game of life
Is too bad to accept,
When the happiest love & the saddest hate
Both together intercept

Being in peace with self here
Is the only important key,
Cheers my friend, to yours and
Some of My JOURNEY! ❤

A PHOTOGRAPH

While we walk this life
Some moments are unforgettable,
We still keep them in our heads,
Even if they are terrible

It's all about a click
A click into the vibes of happiness,
The times when we laughed
To the times when we reach its highness…

The feeling of togetherness
Is so significant,
Words are few to describe
This acceptance is so different

Lots of memories it holds
Even if one is far away,
Looking at some samples
Gives us a reason to stay…

A collection of smiles
Hits so hard, when one is alone,
Even if far away
We have a similar tone

The emotions of people
Reach a place so high,
Where they want to be loved
With the nigga's they wanna touch the sky!

It's all about a frame
To be remembered forever,
Without which, our life would just be a half
Some lines for that Lovely PHOTOGRAPH!
Some lines for that Lovely PHOTOGRAPH! ♥

A LOVELY MEMORY

The world spins round
With some nearing stars,
Yes, a different world
With many beautiful scars

A world full of colors,
With so many pretty smiles,
But you need to keep yours
This time for a while…

The silence is the magic
Of this mystic dark,
It does affect us
Giving us our trademark!!

The stories of love
Are just stories…
But a poor heart is silently
Holding some unforgettable memories….

The letters of an untied thought
Ran far away somewhere,
Into deep words that are
Too beautiful to share

Blessings from divine
In a lovely puzzled way,
I believe someday I reach
A place where I finally stay

My heart feels a lot
But words cover a mile
Keeping this as a short memory
I'll end this someday in my Style...!!

Things that exist but you can't see:

People thinking about you and smiling
Flowers growing within your heart,
The moon's affection for you,
How much you've healed already
A lovely future written in the stars...

Yes, we exist from them....

SCHOOL DAYS

In this big and lucky life,
With so many different phases in it,
We were blessed to have,
Such a time at least for a bit

The times when we were so true
To experience this thunder,
When we never knew about life
& its beautiful wonders!!

The starting prayer to the end ring
We all were connected to one string,
We didn't realize to play it then
But now it's most the playful thing,
In your mind, yeah!!

Growing a little older
Chasing after our dream,
Hustling in this world sometimes
We miss that colorful theme

The last bench tales
Those are never-ending stories,
It is the most remembered time of life
When we made little histories

The essence of an unmatured love
Had its wings to grow,
Hiding from the company sometimes
We always tried to run it slow

The grounds of PT sessions
Took us to a lively mood,
When everything was misbalanced
But still, we stood by our hood
Those little moments on our bench
Are still remembered by this mind,

Yes! Life was so precious in those moments
When we were one of a kind!!

Walking this life now
Everyone has their own goal,
So beautiful was the time
When we all were one soul

Traveling to explore this world
We reached so far away,
I am so grateful to have
Such schoolmates on my way

Thankful to everyone
To show some existence,
We all are one but
Until my last sentence

One out of you,
Which turned out to be a Poet
Remembering my school days
Yes, it was my favorite moment

Even if we are far away
That blackboard pulls you back
Gathering some memories for life
Getting back to the shack!!!!!

Yes, cheers to the Magical School Days ♥

GROW

In this huge fast world
Running, a bit slow,
Matching with its speed
Don't forget to GROW

Even if it feels sad
Heartbreaks in a row,
Know your worth and
Don't forget to GROW

Thoughts flying high
Sometimes very low,
Be wise to choose them for a while, but
Don't forget to GROW

With a bunch of blessings
& some feelings to throw,
Always believe in yourself but
Don't forget to GROW

Look at the stars
See how they glow,
Illuminating ourselves from within
Don't forget to GROW

There's a lot to learn
& A lot to know,
Realizing these two things
Don't forget to GROW

Everyone surviving here
Must change for better & GROW,
Because this is Life, my friend
No retakes, no rewinds
Just a one-time show..!!

GOOD OLD DAYS

Years ago, before this day
We didn't know little, about our way,

We were so busy, with people and their smiles,
Which made us forget, our worth for a while

Love and love was all around
Happiness was the only friend, which used to surround

Sometimes good, sometimes bad,
Cheers to those moments, which we never really had

We always believed life is so best,
And thank GOD for such a wonderful quest!

Plenty of nights, to cherish and recall,
Do you remember the memories, created by all?

A blessed phase of life
Can be described in million ways
Something about those
Crazy,

GOOD OLD DAYS..!!

YES, I AM WAITING!!

From the wonders of joy
To the times when I was alone,
Grateful for this life &
For the things it has shown

Living like a free bird
Flying like an eagle,
Higher and higher I go
Sometimes it's just unstoppable

The summary of those stories
Are too vast to be explained,
Missing home, My Whole Heart
Waiting for the moments that never came

Came to my mind,
With a shot of whiskey & wine,
Someday I will show them'
How to beautifully shine

This is all that we got
Some days are just easy to recall,
While some days show you
How can one rise, when everything falls...!!
Searching for happiness
Surviving this lovely period,
My heart has already turned black
Waiting for it to turn Red!

Yes, I am Waiting...!! ♥

The deep touch of words
With a little magic of ink
Shows you something
When one is far away
It teaches a new way of life
& the things that could forever stay....

Waiting to return
Return to my dreams & a lot....
Waiting for a miracle
Which I never thought!

YES, I AM WAITING...!! ❤

TALKING LIFE

The earth spins round, in a silent sound,
And so do me, to set you free…

The childhood calls and the raindrops fall,
Playing in the mud, till becoming a young stud

Then I turn the cards, till deadly miles & yards,
So that you get lost, at any cost…

People change, Feelings fade,
Things go wrong, and Memories remain…

Struggling through broken dreams, maybe it's too late it seems,
I never stop, if you're a hit or a flop

Refreshed minds and growing needs,
Birth of new thoughts, either of good deeds

At last, all sets, with a thumbs up,
Leading to one's destiny
Hey, this is LIFE...ssup?

LET'S TALK.... ♥

BRIGHT LIGHT

Even if you are going
Through the deadly storms,
Remember, someday you'll be happy
In many different forms…

Just believing in this
Will not work much,
You'll have to push it, my friend
At least give it a touch

Many things behind you
Are just about to turn,
You'll have to work hard
You should be ready to burn…

Burn a little bit,
For the heart that beats,
It creates Magic...
In the streets of love, with a little trip!

Everyone is walking here
It's been a long day,
You'll have to fly high
And just stay away

A lot in yourselves
You've got to do,
Search for the plan &
Make it come true

Follow your soul &
Feel the things that are right,
Because after every dark
There's always a BRIGHT LIGHT! ♥

SUPERMOON

God created this universe
No matter how far,
Yet you shine the brightest
Most beautiful star!!

Every planet has its own
A different name,
But no one knows yours
From where it came?

Has its glow
And a role to play,
The magic to catch every eye
What more can we say?

An amazing light
Helps the earth shine,
Staring at you
Can make one feel fine…

Sometimes half
Sometimes full,
No matter what
You always look bloody cool

Why do we watch everything?
Up above in the sky,
Even if we don't know
But only in the night, oh why?

Spending the day well
Waiting for it to turn soon,
With a hope to watch you again
This one's for the SUPERMOON...!!
Feel it!

It Speaks to You..!! ♥

HUGS

The only best thing
In our life,
Which always makes us feel
A little alive!

Sometimes in love
Sometimes in pain,
It amuses me that people
Does not remain the same…

Filled with emotions
When feelings overflow,
That's the first thing to do
Even if someone feels low…

It's the best feeling
Or just the happiest action,
Which can take you miles far
Just within a fraction

Full of happiness
And sometimes tears,
Deep down inside
A little heart fears

The best thing for one
To just get lost,
The best feel
When memories cross

Things worth remembering
Either sober or on drugs,
This is all about
Those Unforgettable "HUGS"

DO YOU REMEMBER SOME?
Because I do..!!

I am SOMETHING, I am SOMEONE

I am somebody
In the world of everyone,
I am something
I am someone!

I am someone whose mind wants to explore without being stuck,
Whose heart is beating, but wants to feel the beat,
Who wants to just travel without any destination,
Who wants to be loved without any kind of condition…
I am something
I am someone,
Who wants to be desired without being known,
Who wants to fly without having wings,
Who wants to feel every day of winter without letting it go
Whose blood is flowing in the body, but want to feel its flow!
I am something
I am someone,
Whose running behind visions without any purpose,
Who wants to be happy without getting hurt,
Who wants to taste the rain without getting wet,
Who create memories but want to repeat the whole set,
Who am I...?
Just a human being??
With some imaginary thoughts
No, that's not true or false!

I am somebody,
In the world of everyone
I am something
I am someone!

YES, YOU ARE...!!

YOU & I (ONE BODY)

There was a time,
When you and I,
Used to be shining stars
Together,
In each other's eyes...

Yes, this feeling of one
Takes the peace away,
I wish you had a reason
Just to smile and stay!

Your kisses hurt like thorns
My body is the one to bear,
Our story is history now
If someone could just hear

The moments when you,
Always stood by my side,
It turned out to be a mystery
When no one was ever beside

Struggling from my gut
Now my heart just bleeds,
Searching for a place where
It could plant the love seeds

Your smile, your presence
Had a different essence,
Which is so hard to find
Also easy to rewind because,
I remember,

"OUR LOVE WAS ONE OF A KIND"

Those promises that keep me alive
I miss you my cutest teddy,
Exploring the world, I feel
How You and I Were Just One Body!

I remember...!! ♥

THE FIRST TIME I SAW YOU

The first time I saw you,
Felt like someone had come
Felt like I had forgotten everything,
And was just ready to overcome...
To overcome the bad times I was falling for,
To those good times, I could hear calling!
Those eyes, glitter
That smile shines
A little angel from paradise,
Just beautiful like my rhymes…
Where were you these days?
I was so alone...
Now that you've come, I can see
Someone of my own,
Though we met before,
I don't remember a bit of it
What if it was meant for now,
So easy and gentle to exhibit…
We met in the dreams,
But this is the first time I saw you
Felt like we had met before
Felt like I was waiting for this view
Was written in our destinies…
To meet in life and the future
This feels a bit high,
& also, a bit of Nature!
People do have a bad habit
Of leaving in between,
I am not good at goodbyes darling,
So do return to this screen
Because,
This is the first time I saw you
Seems like my mind flew,
Somewhere away,
I believe we could be A Great Crew!

HAPPINESS... WE WERE WE!

Someone said, "Happiness looks good on you", but
The reality of Life is you cannot be happy all the time!

Hey hi....... Happiness here!
I am the future of your smile,
And also, the friend of sadness,
I bring joy to people,
And wander their minds to places
The energy in people is unique,
With their different chases......
I am meant to create good times
And also, the unforgettable ones,
Lots of memories hold
Which cannot be described in words...
But my mate is a drop from the eye
Vice-a versa it goes round and round,
After coming so far
Still touched to the ground...
Yeah, indeed, you cannot be happy all the time
Coz it's a feeling and not a mood,
All that does right is,
A pizza and some delicious food
Some shots of tequila
Reminds us all of those days,
When we were young, wild & free
Still trying to climb the life's tree...
But also, sometimes they take you,
To your beloveds,
Writing art, just like the same,
No name, no game
Still galaxies in a frame,

It's about something in the heart
Which always remained unsaid…!!
The story is about how much you care,
Spreading magic everywhere…

Life is not so easy,
Just the way you think it is,
I (happiness) am just a friend here,
Beware of my enemies….
I come in waves, my friend
And there is nothing constant,
Struggling in the sea of freedom
Praising myself very instant..
I come with so many worries
& Also, a lot of apologies,
The magic lies in the emotion
And then the rest are just stories….
Let's overcome these chapters
Which are untold & a bit broken,
Because I (happiness) am with you now &
Things are about to get golden…

Someone said, "Happiness looks good on you", but
The reality of Life is you cannot be happy all the time!
Yeah, yeah yeah!!!!!

Cheers to the time when you were mine,
Swirling around the time shift key
I am, grateful for all the blessings
& also, the time when We Were WE...!!

Someone said, "Happiness looks good on you...!!" ♥

NATURE

A circular world
With the taste of God,
Has its beauty
Both even and odd

Those huge mountains with beautiful rivers
& the shining sky
Do they Have a bond?
With the creatures that fly

They talk and play
A magical unheard tune,
In the night
For the beautiful moon

I love this nature
Which gives me a natural high,
Even I don't know the reason
Should I really care? Why?

The trees they talk
And hide in the fog,
Telling us some stories
Of brutal ghosts and forever glories

Those flowing oceans
With the shiny sunset light,
Teaches us every time
How to shine even more bright

No one or no words
Can describe this miracle,
Years or even in the future
Some lines from my heart
For This Spiritual NATURE...!!

THE MAHADEV

In this big world
People have so many,
But I always have him
& so, I don't need anybody

The creator of this universe
Has his own name
And about his powers?
It goes out of the frame

He is an amazing artist
And also, the peacemaker,
Of this undefined &
Wealthy heart-touching nature

A snake on his neck
& bhasma over the body,
A Trishul to destroy the evil
He is the father of everybody,
Even if the storms come
One by one
Don't worry the third eye,
Keeps a watch on everyone…

The lord of spirituality
Worshipped by all,
With his magical infinities
He catches the one who falls

In my heart, he lives
& not in any cave,
God of Gods
Something for MY MAHADEV...!!

SOMETHING IS WAITING

Now-a-days every day
A thought full of hope,
Revolves around my mind
Crawling through an unknown rope!

Life is tough, but
Staying alone for peace
Will lead you to places,
Where the sun and ocean kiss…

So unpredictable is this theme
In which I am living right now,
Living the life, I want
Surviving this feeling anyhow

Flowing like an ocean,
Through the beautiful sunsets
Passing like a laser through my eyes,
Seems like everything's just met

Transforming into a little minion
Full of love and thoughts,
Thinking out loud with some
Memories and liquor shots

They say, life changes...
Is that for real?
Yes, it is, Just like Magic
Happening just to heal…

Master the Art of Healing
Which will change your life someday,
& If it does not then, maybe
Something is Waiting for You to stay!

"The best relationship in this universe is with the person inside You, and the rest is nature.."

WEEK BY THE DAYS SO HIGH!!

Week by the days so high
Week by the days so high
You by the day, oh why?
I guess until we reach the sky…

Walking this life every time
Thinking someday will be my,
Lots of flowers gazing at the moon
Shivering with the cold winds,
The coast full of golden shadow
Waiting for the dawn very soon,
Let the dreams tell you
What is wrong or right,
Not everyone gets this
What I have got to write,
Love, Love, and love
What is the secret behind this word?
Flowing like water in my blood
Traveling like an eagle around the world,
Let it be your life or thy
Week by the days so high
Week by the days so high ♥

A huge wave shines
Into the deep dark oceans so bright
The nature of a Stargazer
Leads to an epiphany, so right!!
Up in those mountains
There lives a crazy ass boy,
How did he go up there?
Or did he just touch the sky?

Floating in the air with a lovely serene
Catching the shiny dewdrops,
The grass is always greener on the other side
Same as the value of teardrops!

Still, why is the week, by the days so high?

Someone gave birth to a new one
There's an echoing happy cry,
Laying down under the moon's shadow
Thinking out loud in the open mighty sky!
Sitting in an endless virtue
With a glass of thoughts half-filled,
Dancing are the clouds up there
Oceans are about to get thrilled…
Holding your breath by keeping an eye
The days by this week
Be so high ♥
The nature is so beautiful
Keeping all my secrets now,
I am so fearless with this high
It sings me a melodious lullaby...

Yes, it's a Whiskey lullaby,

Life is all about the days and weeks
Which we keep in our hearts till we die,
I don't know about the world!
But these times will always be Mine!! ♥

Some lines for our Life or My,
Week by the days so high ♥

IN MY DREAMS, WHEN I SLEEP AT NIGHT

In my dreams
When I sleep at night,
I find myself searching,
For that never-ending light

A light that I often think off
When I am awake,
For the things which I desire
And the days which I will make!!

The future is not in anyone's hands
You'll grow when you realize this,
It all depends on you
Feeling sorry for the moments you missed!

Live every moment &
Laugh out loud,
Because one day you gonna shine
And make yourself proud...

The days like beautiful sunsets,
Followed by the ashes falling
The smoke playing with the wind
Traveling with your mind thinking,
To make a garden of roses,
Realising the thorns hurt so bad
Hurting is the new love now,
Even if it makes you feel sad...

The magic of newness,
Is so Magical…just take a feel,
My love is already dead but growing
For myself and also to heal

Some days it felt like autumn
Some days like spring,
The seasons keep changing
Just to find that thing…

A ring, a ring of love
In the garden of hope
Surrounded by beautiful red roses
Shining under the moonlight
I find myself searching
When I sleep at night,
In my dreams...!! ♥

TIME CHANGES EVERYTHING (माया)

It's said,
Time changes everything...
Inner wounds don't get healed,
You get used to it...
You learn to live with it...
Building a wall around yourself...
Pushing people away
Because there's a doubt about
Will someone really stay...??
Afraid to be alone
When they go a little far,
Or to love someone
Just like a falling star...

Turning the attitude fearless
Not caring a bit,
Because there's nothing left to lose
Either to quit...
Doubting the intentions of everyone
Defending ourselves
Damaging the one,
Who you thought would damage itself...
Trusting is the new risk
Which you take in,
Resulting to lose faith in people
& also the black days to begin!
Broken by heart
Trying to hurt others too,
Growing stronger day by day
You still don't reveal the Real you...

But there are some people
Who can see through your soul,
Learning from your behavior
Loving your role,
They are all different
Just learn to differentiate,
Everyone does not come here with
A Lovely heart so great!!

But only some remain forever
Watching you on your worst side,
By bringing the good in you &
Just by always staying beside...

Someone said it right
Time changes everything!
Oh yes,
TIME REALLY CHANGES EVERYTHING!! ♥

AN EMPTY HEART!

I tried to be something that I can
I was always afraid of ending up with nothing,
I thank God, that he made you a part of the plan
Of everything which is now, just something…

I thank God, that he made me a stronger man
For the things through which I was going,
Which came out to be a twist in my life
Through the things, back then, I was doing…

Thinking about myself & the old me
The time in which we were not strangers,
But We were We!
Grateful every day for those hands who,
Held me while I was finding the Magic Key!

A key to the dream
Where we are on a clear blue water beach
Sand dunes crippling our bodies
& minds are too far to reach

Sunsets, Endings & Bright rays
Watching them we fell into each other's arms
And disappeared somewhere into the ocean of love
Unexplored, Unknown & Unfound.

Still, I feel your heartbeats
Under the silent moonlight,
With a cup of coffee in my hand
A Pen and paper, just doing things right

Love is like,
A beautiful river of red roses flowing in the dark,
Very few understand its color and can swim through it,

The moon shining on it as a pearl of hope,
In the eyes of a disguised lover just for a bit…
Life now seems like a beautiful gift
Which still needs to be unpacked,

To laugh often,
To live again,
To love forever ….

LIVING LIFE!

**Carrying myself every day
Talking to myself
Tripping on myself
Dancing with myself!
All this came by the Grace of God
This is an amazing race,
Praising myself,
Learning from myself
Still standing with confidence
Now, this is a coincidence,
The moon is high up above
Shining from the black space
All you need is the light
Just to travel & escape!
Thinking out loud
This is just a chase...
A test of how far….
How far you have come
From the unforgotten years
Nothing is just the same!!**

**Look at You, yes you,
You used to wait for someone,
Many strangers passed by
But I am still here waiting for the one…
We feeling up tonight
Doing all right, we don't really care,
What happens tomorrow
But there is something that always makes us scared!
Traveling with time
In the winds of desire,
Its presence is just, in its absence
Felt, but never missed !!
The heart stories, yes
The heart stories…
Someone else when they stay,
Writing miracles, Creating histories**

Every day seems to be different,
Finding yourselves,
In this unsolved yet magical story
Things I kept to myself...
Are the ones that trouble
But healing from distractions,
Is a key to success
In so many ways & situations...!!
Keep walking & finding,
What is meant for you
Keep chasing your dream if you have any,
Because living for it here are so many...!!

What to conclude and say
Everyone is just a little magic,
Here to live a legacy,
A pen fighting with the ink,
In the ocean of hope,
Everything just sank...!!
Let go of what is gone
Cheers to now & here on…
We made it here,
Through everything and just beyond…

Dying every day but living forever
Words are not enough to say
This feeling is amazing,
I want this to stay...
Carrying myself every day
Talking to myself
Tripping on myself
Dancing with myself!

LIVING LIFE!! ❤

ON THE OTHER SIDE OF LIFE..!!

On the other side of life,
Yes, On the other side of life
Who knows what it is?
A world of darkness & love?
Maybe both, a little bit,

So much of energies
All living with a hunger,
To go back to life
A lost world for a new stranger…

A heaven of great people
Full of love and good deeds,
Who knows when one can go
To plant the afterlife seeds

We all live with fear here,
A fear of missing a moment or dying in it
Well, on the other side
It's all peaceful and lit

Who knows how they live
With incomplete love & dreams,
Sometimes I think, the voices we hear at night
Are there unheard screams...

They live on the other side,
The heroes of mankind
Respect to them for the examples
They have set in the world,
Which are so hard to find…

Living here right now,
Live every moment,
Because someday,
You will also remember yourself,

ON THE OTHER SIDE OF LIFE...!!

THIS IS FOR YOU

MEMORIES

The things we live on
The things we do praise,
Sometimes they act to us like
Bright sunshine rays...
These are the memories
Whom we cherish the most
Something is staying back
Along this lovely coast…
Mind remembers everything
But the heart still cries
No matter where you are
Let it be the skies…
A time comes to walk
In this unpredictable future,
To Chase your desire
& rest is just nature
Thousands of moments
Create a different vibe,
Be thankful for every bit
Just enjoy the free tribe…
It feels so blessed
To write in this beautiful sky,
It's just a matter of thought
The reason is still unknown, oh why?
Follow your faith
And your dreams too,
Because Dreams bring back the Memories
And the Memories bring back You! ♥

SOME DEEP PEOPLE

Everyone here
In their life's game,
Are so busy to create
Self-empire & their own name

The road goes up
And sometimes down,
They always move with it
No matter in any country or town

They have a lot
To listen & to say,
But words turn less
And so do the days

Thinking some more
On the mind-blowing thoughts,
Tons of memories
They've already caught

Living life to the fullest
And every moment of it
They know somewhere back
Where exactly to commit

Exploring themselves
In a very different form,
They know the truth very well
And a way to transform
WHO ARE THEY?
The journey to their heart
Does not really need much diesel,
You are very close to them
These are SOME DEEP PEOPLE!

FIND THEM & KEEP THEM....!!

THE OLD YOU

In a world full of love
As we grew older,
Surviving so many years
Living life stronger and bolder

The dilemma of getting young
Took us incredibly high,
We flew away with it
And tasted the glowing sky….

Caught up nowadays,
In a jungle called "Life"
Struggling with the groove &
Learning new things to survive

The love that we have
In our falling and failing hearts,
Is an expensive treasure, my friend
Coming from the past, including its part!!

Memories are the bright stars
In our vast and beautiful blues,
We had an epiphany once
& than we ran out of clues

Grateful for the journey of life,
Rocking' some ways in the darkness,
Turning out to be a cold play now,
Leaving behind some moments speechless..

A Rush of Blood to the Mind
Makes it a vibe to see through,
A feather dipped in the golden ink
Describing some of THE OLD YOU!

DO YOU MISS..?? ❤

LIFE OF A LOVER

So complicated is the Life of a Lover,
Beginnings, Feelings
Tripping's and Endings...
Start to a new life in between,
While we reach that thing
It is already Spring,
But Life is a ring,
Full of twists and turns
The one who lives it
Is always ready to burn…
Without a single wing, he tries to fly high,
With a perfect swing, in this beautiful sky...
The meaning of this life is so hard to learn
The one who survives enjoys the run...

Millions of thoughts do come and go away
Where she leaves her place
But still, He stays………
He stays in this life
Touching the illusion
With a creative future
In his own perception!!
Memories of happiness & full of love
Do the rest of the thing
This aesthetic evening……
Two shots of tequila
Was it a perfect ending?
No one knows the mystery, nor the hidden story
Maybe, He knows it!
Because He is the hero,
Which was turned to zero,
Knowing his value, he travelled this thought
Believing in his unknown path……
He dreamed of the moon in the daylight
Which always gave him
A reason to stay!!
Although his moon was already lost
He didn't give up, at any cost...

He is the one,
Who loved the most every time
Can someone Love him?
Not forever, but for some time...
This life is so different, which he never dreamt off
So tough was the feeling for him
To let her go off...

The Life of a lover is not so bad,
It's complicated though...
We never know when someone can go through it
No matter what, Just LOVE YOURSELF &
Never give up!
We all exist today in this world, only
Because of the love in our hearts in many
Different forms!!
Because always remember,

Love is what wins in the End!! ❤

A to Z OF MY LIFE

A child born in a city of dreams,
Beginning the journey called Life
Crying sometimes, which was never a habit
Doing everything just as his type…
Everyone around him smiles
Feels to just get lost by
Getting to see new things for a while….
Having nothing even when it was everything,
Imagination had its wings,
Just to feel the magic
Knowing some truths of life & also,
Learning some secrets that were
Meant to survive!
Nothing worked then either,
Out of love and decisions,
Present makes all the difference here,
Quitting all the past perceptions!
Reaching a place to stay,
Searching for that lovely feeling,
Treating himself with extra love
Unique is the moment in which he's living 🖤
Violet as the dark blue
Which turns out to be a clue
Xperiencing the throwback of those nights
You and him, was really his favorite view!
Zero is the square of zero

Only If He could be your Hero!
Yes, I am your Hero! 🖤

A FALLING STAR

In this big universe
Holding N' number of galaxies and stars,
Millions of them survive here
But only a few stay with fear...

The one who fails to stick around
To the heavenly sky,
Loose's it's relation with it
And is thrown away to fly

To fly and catch a human eye
Asking for their lovely wish or a prayer,
To the eternity from where it left
When everything was just over....

I hope it makes the wishes come true
Of those who are eager for something,
Believing in themselves and
Rest is just a hopeful thing

For the dreams that are felt
And the thoughts desired,
This feeling is amazing
Which keeps up the fire

Keeping the hope alive
In this beating heart,
With an amazing energy to touch it
Fulfilling many ways to start....

What if it fulfills the wish of those
Who were once together but are now very far,
Maybe it knows the pain of falling
Yes, this is for The FALLING STAR!! ♥

ALONE

Sometimes so busy
& sometimes so free,
In these times, there are some things
No one, but only I can see

Surviving this life, now in the present
Living with a different emotion,
It makes me so high
Feels like, I am sinking in a thoughtful ocean…

This feeling takes me there
Where I can see no one but only me,
I often think about
How mismatched were we!

It takes a lot to survive
When your heart is bleeding out of pain,
Trust me, my friend,
This is the time when you will really gain

Gain a mind to think
What we truly deserve,
Yeah, Memories are just love,
Which can only be preserved...

The essence of nothing
From your loved ones & the beloved past,
Helps you to grow by
Giving the things that you never asked….

These moments are unprecedented
In which, one is always unknown,
Still burning more in this fire,
For the times when I was "ALONE"

"ALONE TO BE REALLY KNOWN" ♥

WITNESSING MIRACLE

One moment to live
One moment to die
One moment to remember
& one moment to cry ♥
One moment of sunset
Where I met you,
Somewhere in the universe
I still don't have a clue
Standing beside the Ocean,
Waves talking to the soul
Shining on them is the future
Just for a moment or maybe a whole
I am still here,
Spending time in this beauty
Sipping a little fruity
Missing you, my cutie...
Thought of reaching the depth,
But I don't know how to swim
One moment of wonder
& just the other, I win....
Butterflies flying in the forest,
Spreading colors of love,
I am wandering here,
Carrying so much to show
On a Christmas night,
When Santa brought You to Me...
I am still confused here...
Stitching love with a silver needle...
One moment to love,
One moment to hate,
One moment to share
& one moment for the limitless care ♥
Finding woods in this jungle of life,
To fire the endless hope
Having a cup of black coffee together
But there's hardly any scope...

There are those who walk,
There are those who run,
We are the fortunate ones here
But for a moment we are none...!!

Feeling the vibe of these winds
With a beautiful sunset,
There is no moment here
Until one fights & then sweats....
Fighting to win,
We are here but not the same,
This is not a moment, my friend
This is the Whole game...!!
One moment to fall
One moment to stand
Just to rise up from this mess
Without a helping hand...
Sounds of these birds, they ask you
Some melodious questions
But talking to the mountains
Will heal so many situations...!!
About the memories,
Cheers to the never-ending life
Where we are one,
And some are just done!!
This is the moment now,
Every thought you can better think off
One moment for self-love
One moment to live forever
In that moment we live beyond
Followed by the other...
Someone said the show must go on
And it is Indeed....
Writing some lines of motivation
For myself and you too
Because together we are here!
Witnessing this miracle for free! ♥

DEFINITELY, I AM WAITING...!!

Once upon a time in life,
When you were, a part of it
Just like a film of love
Which turned out to be a Superhit…
Your kisses and your hugs,
Where are the best times?
Writing poetry every day, but still,
They were more peaceful than my rhymes,
Let that body be one,
With a mixture of souls twice,
This life is not equivalent
Just as to play with some dice...
If two bodies could be one,
Is this even possible?
Still, I find your existence
In my dreams and its phenomenal...
Two energies in one soul,
Two people, in one body,
I always imagined if,
I could be better than anybody...
The frequency of our hearts
Which was unmatchable sometimes,
Turned out to be a miracle now
Which was a gift at those times…
The flower of love,
Was the prettiest in our garden,
Memories are just like fog
And everything is just raw……

Don't know why my Love Life,
Makes me stand again in this present
The future is just unpredictable
Searching for both of us on my way....
Even after years,
The heart will still hold this
Who knows if everyone is aware off,
What they never want to miss......
In this truthful path of life
It's so hard to forgive the truth,
As the weather turned its face

Heartlessly, so did you..................
But the time when I was yours,
And you were mine...
Still keeps me awake at night
With millions of thoughts which is just fine...

Don't know why sometimes
It feels like I am dead,
Waiting for a miracle instead
Which is out of my head..

Definitely, I am Waiting...!! ♥ ♥

YOU ARE A PLAYER

There's a difference in those
People who live for themselves,
& Amongst all who live for others
Forgetting their own self

The real gold is never found
It's just unique in itself,
All the things you wish for
They are already in yourself..!!

Try searching them
For many people who did....
The feeling after finding them'
Will take you back to being a kid

Afraid of losing it
Acting weird sometimes,
These daysssss & et cetera......
I wish I had some more time

Some more time for
Every moment of my life
For those who regret
Remember! There's never a rewind

For all the legends who stayed
And did what they wanted to,
Leaving a legacy behind
A story so real & true...!!

Yes, you are amongst those few
Living the best in the present,
Doing what you want to
For the things which are meant...

Great people do what they want
But you can do, what you can't,
The secret of this life is
Which you never found...

Try to find it in yourself
And then everywhere around
This is life, my friend!
YOU ARE A PLAYER &
Rest is just a playground!

SPECIAL..!!

One day staring at the mirror
I felt, there was so much to explore
Giving yourself lakhs of attention
Will surely give you, A crore!
All these lines are not motivational
There lies a truth,
UNKNOWN TO SO MANY HERE!!

Feeling blessed to know it
Praising every day & every year..
Walking & Writing a Miracle,
UNKNOWN TO SO MANY HERE!!

Loving yourself will reveal,
Magic & some unknown fears!
Tears, they come from the sky
From the broken clouds,
Never did they know
They would strike, cry & then fly...!!
There's a thunder, up above in the sky
Thrashing with the light of hope
Reached a place somewhere,
UNKNOWN TO SO MANY HERE!!

Full of stars, what a sight...
Be ready to fight,
Only you can defend yourself
Just by following your right...!!
There are a bunch of secrets
You'll find if you try to search
These are the blessings
You won't get from any church!

The moon is high up above
Shining from the vast black space
UNKNOWN TO SO MANY HERE,
Is this life's amazing race!!

Every struggle matters here
From lunch till the metro days,
Destiny always has a plan
To open up in so many ways...

One day staring at the sky
I felt, there was so much to explore
Tried to touch it though
But it takes a lot more...!!
Walking & writing in my style
Looking at this beautiful nature,
This is something different,
STILL UNKNOWN TO SO MANY HERE!!

SPECIAL...!!!!

A POET, AN ANOTHER LIFE..!!

A POET, AN ANOTHER LIFE!!

From the good minds and some little trip
Taking it sip by sip,
The water of becoming something
Which flew away into words so deep,
The body does not decide it
Nor some people who are different,
It is a blessing to live like this
Down here now in the present....
I never thought I could write something,
Which would touch people's hearts
But, Cheers to those who have
Lived together and then were apart...
Let it be a poem or a story
It out-speaks the feeling of a life,
Which lived beneath these blue skies
And then the rest is just magic!!
A magician of words,
Creating an emotion to feel,
To live once again in this world,
To be remembered as someone who heals...
Healing through life, living some diversions,
Traveling to places,
Where I found a person..!!
A person whom I live by,
A person who is out of my mind,
A person who completely knows me,
A person who is one of my kind,

Yes, he is another person
The POET in ME!!
Feels lucky to live two lives
I have the other's key!!

It feels like I write myself & my heart out
Jumbling and playing with words,
Trying to deliver a connect
To reach out to one's soul,
This life is so beautiful
Just to relate and touch a feeling,
I have been through those times,
When I was unable to find a living…
But then I found a purpose
To live, to grow, and to embrace,
And also to write something,
Which could help me reach my place
My friend,
I call it Heaven's crest...
Sometimes it's just a bond with myself
Which never gets too old
I believe it's real
Hell yeah! It's similar to Real Gold
Proud of myself
For the things which I write,
In the meanwhile,
The future seems to be right & bright

Yes, this is another person,
A hidden poet in me,
Trying to talk to the stars,
Where I once saw, WE...!!
And then,
❤ *Rest is just LIFE...!!* ❤

Acknowledgments

Thank you, Mom & Dad, for always supporting me for so many years to chase my dream and for the freedom you gave me. To keep the front doors, open & go beyond to learn more & more about life & support my passion for writing.

Thank you to my teachers from my school (Don Bosco) for teaching me to learn this language so that I could write my book someday & also Thank you British Council, Connaught Place, New Delhi for some wonderful courses & for the insights into the English language which helped me improve my poetry and writing, the teaching staff, the examination team & my colleagues for being so humble & supportive throughout.

What should I say about my elder brother, thank you for always being the backbone, for giving so much & for always reading my poetry & sharing your valuable feedback on it. It always motivated me to write more & more, also my sister-in-law is so supportive all the time of whatever I do like a real sister. Thank you, guys!!

Thank you to all my friends who always keep my wine glasses constantly topped up.

And another big thank you to all my lovely readers.

Love you all.

Thank you

I wrote this book alone, but it was a journey in which you & I both travelled together.

Although it's time to part ways, I am sure we will meet again.

Maybe back at the beginning of Two Hearts Never Heal the Same.

After all, it was written to read more than once—on some beautiful mornings & sunsets, sitting beside the oceans, on the mountain tops, with some coffee on rainy days & some amazing sleepless nights.

See you soon in my next book, until then please be in touch & feel free to share your thoughts and photographs with me. I would love to feel you when you read my poetry.

Facebook—Bhushan Gosavi (My Page: The Lively Poet)
Instagram—bhushiii (thelivelypoet)

Thank you for your time & reading this book. I wish you lots of love in your life...!!

I believe in you...!!

KEEP DREAMING, DREAM BIG...!!

www.ingramcontent.com/pod-product-compliance
Lightning Source LLC
LaVergne TN
LVHW091304150826
845673LV00006B/1534

9789334058352